THE LLANGOLLEN RAILWAY IN THE LATE TWENTIETH CENTURY

Doug Birmingham

AMBERLEY

First published 2019

Amberley Publishing
The Hill, Stroud
Gloucestershire, GL5 4EP

www.amberley-books.com

Copyright © Doug Birmingham, 2019

The right of Doug Birmingham to be identified as the Author of this work has been asserted in accordance with the Copyrights, Designs and Patents Act 1988.

ISBN 978 1 4456 8834 3 (print)
ISBN 978 1 4456 8835 0 (ebook)

British Library Cataloguing in Publication Data.
A catalogue record for this book is available from the British Library.

Origination by Amberley Publishing.
Printed in the UK.

Introduction

The Llangollen Railway is acknowledged as one of the premier standard gauge steam railways in the United Kingdom, assisted by it winding through the beautiful Dee Valley in the heart of Denbighshire, North Wales.

The railway has its beginnings with the formation of the Flint & Deeside Railway Preservation Society (FDRPS) in 1972. With the aim of operating a preserved standard gauge line in North Wales, it eventually chose the closed Llangollen station as its base. The station was on the former Great Western line, which used to stretch from Ruabon, Denbighshire, to Dolgellau, Gwynedd, and further on to Barmouth. Sadly, the line from Llangollen to Dolgellau was officially closed in January 1965 with the remainder going east to Ruabon closed in April 1968 when the last freight service ceased to operate. The line was lifted shortly afterwards and the trackbed left for nature to reclaim.

In June 1975, the FDRPS was granted a lease to Llangollen station and went on to restore the location, which saw its first open day on 13 September 1975, where it was warmly received by the 1,500 visitors that attended the event. Between 1975 and 1981, the FDRPS – which reformed into the Llangollen Railway Society in 1977 – set about rebuilding the railway initially as far as Pentrefelin, three quarters of a mile away, which also included various sidings and the ex-goods shed area.

In 1981, the Railway Inspectorate (DoT) passed the track for use with the first passenger train leaving Llangollen station on 26 July. During the same year, the railway was granted a twenty-one-year lease for the 10 miles of trackbed as far as Corwen, which was the planned western terminus. Over the next five years, efforts were then made to extend the track to the first station on the line, Berwyn, 1.75 miles away, and that included the bridge across the River Dee too.

In October 1985, the first passenger train operated to Berwyn, although passengers were initially unable to detrain at the station, which did not happen until March 1986. It was during 1985 that the author became familiar with the railway and the start of many visits to the line up to 2003, hence the title of the book.

In the intervening years in order to reach Carrog, the railway re-laid the sidings into Pentrefelin Sidings, then extended initially to Deeside Halt, which was 3.25 miles from Llangollen station. This included accessing the 689-yard Berwyn Tunnel to reach Deeside Halt. The tunnel is actually the longest single bore tunnel on any preserved line in the United Kingdom. The first passenger trains operated to Deeside Halt was in April 1990, and then the push was on to reach the next destination of Glyndyfrdwy station, a further 2 miles away. Remarkably, this was reached twenty-four months later, with the first trains being operated during April 1992, although the station was not actually fully completed until the following year.

The next target was Carrog station, where the former station was remarkably still intact although the station master's house was now in private ownership. However, before the railway reached Carrog, it was a question of consolidation and improving the existing facilities on the railway. The railway finally reached Carrog – the 'extension', as it was known – and it was officially opened to passenger trains on 2 May 1996. The next goal was to reach Corwen, another 2 miles away, and due to numerous reasons it took nearly twenty years to achieve. However, due to the timespan involved, this section of line is outside the scope of this book.

Regardless, reaching Carrog was no mean feat, especially when you consider the majority of the work was carried out by volunteers in all weathers, which included relaying sleepers, rails, restoring signal boxes and signals, building new stations and restoring existing buildings. However, you need locomotives and rolling stock to operate on the line. In many cases this meant restoring locos from scrap appearance to full working order – especially when they had to raise money to pay for the rebuilding and restorations too. Without those volunteers – along with support from outside organisations, such as Shell UK Oil, British Nuclear Fuels and various public bodies, especially in the early years – there would be no railway.

As the line progressed, the Llangollen Railway was receiving praise from all quarters, not least for the scenic beauty of the Dee Valley. During the years the railway received visits from locomotives such as former BR Class A4 No 60009 *Union of South Africa* and no less than ex-BR Class A3 No. 60103 (4472) *Flying Scotsman,* among many others. The visit of these locomotives raised the profile of the railway even more, attracting visitors from across the UK and also abroad too.

The author became actively involved with the railway during the timespan of this book, which gave him the opportunity to record the progress of the railway, including the numerous ex-British Railways steam and diesel locomotives that visited the line. It is hoped the contents of this book reflect this but also show the scenic beauty of the countryside as the line wanders through the Dee Valley from Llangollen to Carrog.

I would like to express my grateful thanks to many people at the Llangollen Railway and the surrounding area who gave their time, support and assistance in order for me (and others) to obtain some of the images in this book, some of whom became good friends during that period too. However, there are two people without whom I would doubt this book would have been possible. I refer to Chief Mechanical Engineer Dave Owen and Harry Barber of the Carriage & Wagon Department as their unwavering support – and in some instances, sleepless nights – cannot be underestimated. I will always be eternally grateful for their time and efforts.

Finally, I would like to express my personal thanks to my good friend Brian Dobbs, as without his initial encouragement, time and assistance my photographic skills and images would be the poorer. However, without doubt, I would not have completed this book without the support and patience of my wife of forty-two years, Glynis, who has remained my rock and allowed me to indulge in my railway pastime. My very grateful thanks and love in more ways than I am able express.

Doug Birmingham,
Liverpool
December 2018

Taken during the summer of 1984, former Kitson (Leeds)-built 0-6-0T *Austin 1* – now renumbered 5459 and renamed *Burtonwood Brewer* – has just arrived at Llangollen station with a shuttle train from Goods Junction. The locomotive formerly worked at the Austin's Longbridge automotive factory in Birmingham until it was purchased for the Llangollen Railway Society by Burtonwood Brewery, hence the name change in recognition of the brewery's assistance. (Photo: 8A Rail Collection.)

A general view of Llangollen station taken from the road and river bridge with No. 5459 *Burtonwood Brewer* by this time turned to face the other direction, having just arrived at the station. The train comprises two former BR Mk 1 Suburban Coaches, a DMU driving trailer and a former LNER four-wheel Pigeon Van that had been rebuilt into a saloon for disabled people, known as the 'Sunshine Coach'. In the bay platform complete with false chimney is Fowler-built 0-4-0 diesel shunter *Eliseg*. 20 October 1985.

The railway's first ex-BR locomotive visitor was former Great Western 1400 Class No. 1466, a 0-4-2T on loan from the Didcot Railway Centre. It is seen here departing from Llangollen station with the 17.00 train to Berwyn station. The latter station, being 1.75 miles away, was the first station to be reached on the line, with services having commenced the previous March. 7 September 1986.

Another view of Great Western Society 0-4-2T No. 1466, this time crossing the bridge across the River Dee with the 15.00 Llangollen to Berwyn train on 7 September 1986. This location became one of *the* locations on the line to photograph trains and was only possible reach by walking across the river bridge. The bridge, known as Dee Bridge, was repaired by McTay Construction in late 1984 at a cost of £30,000, which was only possible due to a grant and loans from the local council.

Outside the original goods shed in Llangollen yard, Great Western Pannier tank No. 7715, on loan from the Buckingham Railway Centre, is seen in company with former LMS Jinty No. 7298, which arrived at the railway from Steamport, Southport, in 1984. On the right is British Railways Manor class No. 7822 *Foxcote Manor* complete with 'Cambrian Coast Express' headboard outside her own shed. The Manor was under restoration at this time and still some months away from steaming again. 12 September 1987.

Another locomotive on loan from Didcot Railway Centre was Great Western Prairie 2-6-2T No. 5572, which had arrived for a few months in 1988 to assist with promoting the railway to the wider world. Seen here at Llangollen station on 7 August 1988, it is awaiting to depart with the 15.00 train to Berwyn. The former waiting rooms are also visible, which were still awaiting restoration.

Following from the previous image, two people relax and admire No. 5572 as she arrives with her train at Berwyn station. The orange ramp allows disabled people to access the Sunshine Coach, which was normally marshalled on the timetable service trains. The coach was rebuilt with funds from the Sunshine Foundation, hence its name. 7 August 1988.

One of the classic locations on the line is the viaduct and station at Berwyn, which runs alongside the A5 road. Here, newly restored BR Manor class No. 7822 *Foxcote Manor* is about to depart to the loop, 150 yards away, to allow the locomotive to run round the coaches and return to Llangollen tender-first. The station platform and unique building date from when this part of the line first opened, in 1865. The location had become a tourist attraction due to the nearby Horseshoe Falls. 30 May 1988.

Looking immaculate, BR Manor No. 7822 *Foxcote Manor* attacks the climb to Dee Bridge and up Berwyn Bank with the 11.00 Llangollen to Berwyn train on Saturday 9 April 1988. In front of the photographer is the line that runs to the former excursion carriage sidings at Pentrefelin and to the left is the tow/footpath alongside the Llangollen Canal.

A night-time portrait of No. 7822 *Foxcote Manor* taken in Llangollen goods yard on 17 September 1988. This excellent locomotive arrived at the railway in parts from Oswestry during 1985 and over the next three years she was fully restored by volunteers. On Saturday 9 April 1988 she was formally re-dedicated with due ceremony at Llangollen station.

Former Great Western Pannier tank No. 7760 was hired to the railway during 1989 by the Birmingham Railway Museum and was subsequently used on the line's passenger trains to Berwyn. On 15 May 1989, No. 7760 was hired to celebrate my good friend's birthday and hauled a goods train as far as the east entrance of the 689-yard Berwyn Tunnel. This was actually the first steam-hauled train to reach this location since the line was closed in the 1960s. In this view, where the trackbed is still awaiting ballast and with a bed of bluebells in the foreground, the train is posed about 75 yards away from the tunnel entrance.

A contrast in locomotive liveries and which one is correct? In this view, two Manor class locomotives are seen coupled together, the nearest being No. 7828 *Odney Manor* owned by Ken Ryder, which arrived at the railway a few months previously and in an unusual shade of British Railways green. At the front is No. 7822 *Foxcote Manor* in British Railways 'Brunswick Green', which was acknowledge by many as the correct shade of green. With volunteers John Milton (in white shirt) and Ernie Jones on the footplate of *Odney Manor*, the train is waiting to depart Llangollen station with the 15.00 train to Berwyn station. 18 June 1989.

Climbing the last few yards of Berwyn Bank and approaching Berwyn station, No. 7822 *Foxcote Manor*, leading classmate No. 7828 *Odney Manor*, makes a fine sight on a warm summer's evening with the final passenger train of the day during a Gala weekend. No. 7822 is complete with the 'Cambrian Coast Express' headboard, which was a reminder of days gone by when trains travelled to Barmouth. This weekend was the first time that double-headed Manors had been seen on this line since the 1960s. 18 June 1989.

A historic occasion took place on a cold, wet Saturday 6 January 1990 when No. 7828 *Odney Manor* was the first steam locomotive to go through Berwyn Tunnel and onward to Deeside Halt, which was to become the railway's next station on the line after Berwyn. This was a proving run to make sure the locomotive and coaches were in gauge when going through the 689-yard tunnel. It was deemed a success and the train is seen at the Deeside run-round loop, which is still waiting to be bedded in with ballast.

Although the railway was now using ex-British Railways locomotives to haul the line's passenger service, occasionally – and especially on off–peak trains – 0-6-0ST No. 5459 (*Austin 1*) would be put into service. At the time, No. 5459 had been repainted into lined out green livery. Hauling just three coaches, she is working hard as she climbs up Berwyn Bank toward the tunnel entrance on 10 June 1990. In the background is the county house of Bryntysilio Hall, which was the summer residence of Sir Theodore Martin in the late nineteen century.

In April 1990, the first passenger trains operated to Deeside Halt, which was 3.25 miles from Llangollen station. At a location known as Tanners Leap, No. 7822 *Foxcote Manor* with a Great Western 'Siphon' bogie milk van in tow is on the final approach to Deeside Halt with the 17.00 Llangollen passenger train on 10 June 1990.

Having reached Deeside Halt, efforts were now being made to reach the next station on the line – the former Glyndyfrdwy station, 2 miles away. Although the station house still existed (albeit as a private residence) and platform remains were still evident, there was much work to be carried out to reach this location. Initially the railway made its intentions and presence known when it recovered the former GWR Leaton Signal Box and erected the box at Glyndyfrdwy. This was the scene on 10 June 1990, with the signal box in position and concrete sleepers and the water tank waiting to be put into place.

A further 2.5 miles on from Glyndyfrdwy is the former station of Carrog. Taken on the same day as the previous image, this is the view of the closed station looking east. Although reaching this location would be straightforward, the former station house was now in private ownership, and besides the restoration of the track, a signal box, signals and waiting room would have to be built before a train could reach this location.

No. 7822 *Foxcote Manor* is seen crossing Dee Bridge before attacking Berwyn Bank with the 16.20 Llangollen to Glyndyfrdwy train on 14 April 1991. Both the locomotive and the location helped in putting the railway on the map and making Llangollen a more popular location for tourists and railway enthusiasts.

For operational reasons it was unusual to find a locomotive facing east on the line but it is always subject to how it was loaded at its home line, which dictated the direction of the locomotive when it arrived at Llangollen. In this instance, and making a two-month visit from the Severn Valley Railway, former BR Ivatt Class 2 No. 46443 approaches Dee Bridge with the 16.50 Deeside Halt to Llangollen train. This class of locomotive made regular appearances on the line during British Railway days in the early 1960s.

Another locomotive that arrived during autumn 1991 from the Severn Valley Railway was Prairie 2-6-2T No. 4566, which was immediately put into service on the railway. Again the locomotive arrived at the railway facing east and is seen at Berwyn station while participating in a private goods charter on 14 October 1991. The image was set up to show the crew of the train taking a break before we departed to Llangollen station. Left to right: Dave Owen (driver); Bob Haslam (fireman); and Grenville Britland (guard).

Taken from the road bridge that crosses the River Dee and with the assistance of portable floodlights, ex-LMS Jinty No. 7298 and her goods train provide a spectacular view while the train rests at Berwyn station on 2 November 1991. This was only possible due to being a private charter organised by the author and Brian Dobbs, and we had full access to the line, it being a non-operational day.

A view taken from Castle Street bridge which crosses the River Dee in Llangollen showing the station, signal box and covered footbridge – all very much in keeping with its Great Western heritage. Having arrived a few minutes previously, Prairie 2-6-2T No. 4566 is seen with her goods train, which includes two china clay hood wagons that were built during the late 1950s for the china clay traffic originating from Cornwall. 27 March 1992.

On 19 April 1992 and in a lucky patch of sunshine, Severn Valley Railway's Prairie 2-6-2T No. 4566 is highlighted as she rounds the curve at Garth-y-dwr with the 16.42 Glyndyfrdwy to Llangollen passenger train. No. 4566 was built in 1924 at Swindon to the design of G. J. Churchward, who was the Chief Mechanical Engineer at the Great Western Railway at that time.

This image had been given away as a full-size poster by *Railway Magazine* during 1992, but nevertheless is still worthy of being included in this book. Showing the springtime beauty of the Dee Valley, and on a sweeping curve, No. 4566 again works away from Glyndyfrdwy with the 11.47 train to Llangollen on 17 May 1992. In this view, Glyndyfrdwy station is located among the buildings on the mid-right-hand side of this image.

Taken from the station platform and very much out of area, ex-North Eastern Railway Class P3 0-6-0 No. 2392 approaches Glyndyfrdwy Signal Box with the 13.00 train from Llangollen station, while the signalman has his arm out, waiting to collect the single line token from the driver of the train. No. 2392 had only arrived from the North Yorkshire Moors Railway a few days previously and was hired in to cover the passenger service during the summer. 27 May 1992.

This is what No. 2392 was originally built to do – pull goods trains, mainly around the north-east of England. She is seen here hauling eighteen wagons, which was almost the whole operating fleet at that time. The train was a late-running 14.53 Llangollen Goods Junction to Glyndyfrdwy demonstration goods train and was approaching Garth-y-dwr on 3 June 1992. No. 2392 was built at Darlington in 1923 and later became a Class J27 as part of the London North Eastern Railway.

Lit up by portable floodlights and taken from the footplate of ex-LMS Jinty No. 7298, this is a unique view of four other locomotives operating on the railway during the autumn of 1992. From left to right they are: NER P3 0-6-0 No. 2392; ex-BR(W) 2-6-2T No. 4566; ex-BR(W) 4-6-0 No. 7822 *Foxcote Manor*; and ex-BR Standard 4MT 2-6-0 No. 76079. The latter locomotive had only arrived at the railway from the East Lancashire Railway a few days previously. 8 September 1992.

With the arrival of ex-BR Standard 4MT locomotive No. 76079 at the railway, an opportunity was taken to organise a charter hauling a variety of goods wagons, which is seen here passing No. 13 'home' signal after departure from Glyndyfrdwy station. No. 76079 was built by British Railways at Horwich Works in 1957 as part of a class of 115 and spent most of its short working life based in St Helens before withdrawal in June 1967. 2 November 1992.

Taken the same day as the previous image, the beautiful autumn colours of the trees and countryside compliment Standard 4MT No. 76079 and its good train as they come off Dee Bridge, Pentrefelin, on the approach to Llangollen Goods Junction. The wagons in the train included former British Railway four-wheel 12T box wagons as well as various tank wagons that were previously used on the national network.

A scene that could be almost taken in the early 1960s: BR Standard 4MT No. 76079 waits to depart Llangollen station with a goods train to Ruabon! Well, we are able to dream but in reality a scene set up to represent yesteryear to good effect may be? Looking on is the driver of the train, Derek Foster, also the owner of No. 76079, who was a gentleman and a privilege to know, with the signalman in the box being Grenville Britland who had many roles at the railway including signalman, train guard, and ticket collector. 2 November 1992.

Probably the most famous locomotive in the world, No. 4472 *Flying Scotsman* arrived at the railway courtesy of William McAlpine, who was the owner of this iconic locomotive at the time. All was not what it seemed in this image as sadly No. 4472 was declared a failure upon arrival and never actually worked a train during its visit. However, an opportunity was nevertheless taken to pair the locomotive with the railway's prestige dining train, the 'Berwyn Belle', for publicity purposes and they are seen here at Llangollen station on 19 March 1993.

One of the iconic locations on the line is Berwyn station; situated next to the main A5 road, this view shows this magnificent location at its best. The station overlooks the River Dee, and below and crossing the river is the famous Chain Bridge, which connects to the namesake hotel, while in the background are the Berwyn Hills. On 13 March 1993, former LMS Jinty No. 7298 is seen departing with four maroon coaches on the 12.15 Llangollen to Glyndyfrdwy train.

An almost yesteryear scene: a vintage Austin Seven owned by Martin Christie waits to cross the road while Jinty No. 47298 rolls across the crossing to hook up to its goods train before returning to Llangollen. This scene at Glyndyfrdwy was once commonplace across the country in days gone by, and only two years previously you could not have envisaged this would be possible at this location again! 2 April 1993.

Approaching the outer home signal for Glyndyfrdwy station on 2 April 1993, ex-British Railways Jinty No. 47298 steams pass with its short goods train on a private charter. This locomotive was built in 1924 by the London Midland & Scottish Railway and during the 1950s and early 1960s she was based at St Helens Sutton Oak steam shed (8G) in Lancashire, before being withdrawn in early 1967.

The author's daughter and two sons admiring the scenic view of the Dee Valley. In the meantime, ex-LNER Class A4 No. 60009 *Union of South Africa* approaches the station on the last few hundred yards of its journey with the 11.00 train from Llangollen. 4 April 1993.

With the failure of No. 4472 *Flying Scotsman*, John Cameron, the owner of Class A4 No. 60009 *Union of South Africa*, kindly offered to loan the loco to the railway as a substitute. However, before that could happen *Flying Scotsman* had to be hauled to Berwyn Tunnel to test for clearances in the single bore tunnel before the arrival of *Union of South Africa*. The latter is seen here passing Garth-y-dwr on 4 April 1993 with the 15.15 train to Glyndyfrdwy.

In the early 1960s, and before the withdrawal of the Class A4 locomotives, they were regularly used on express trains between Edinburgh and Aberdeen. By coincidence, some parts of the route had similarities to the Dee Valley. In this view, No. 60009 *Union of South Africa* crosses the River Dee at Pentrefelin, providing a 'feel' for those halcyon days with the 12.40 Llangollen to Glyndyfrdwy train on 14 April 1993.

When the members of the Llangollen Railway Society first thought to restore the line, I doubt they would ever have thought a main line-certified ex-LNER Class A4 locomotive might traverse the line, let alone cross the Dee Bridge as in this image. Here, No. 60009 *Union of South Africa* makes light work of its five-coach 16.00 train to Glyndyfrdwy on 14 April 1993.

Ex-BR Standard 4MT Class No. 76079 passes the beautifully restored Llangollen Goods Junction Signal Box with a mixed goods train from Glyndyfrdwy. The signalman waits to receive the single line token from the driver, which will allow another train to enter that section of line in safety. 28 June 1993.

Another visitor to the line was ex-British Railways Standard 4MT Class No. 75029 *Green Knight,* which was based at the East Somerset Railway and owned by famous wildlife artist and conservationist David Shepherd. These locomotives were regular visitors to the line in the early 1960s, and this view is a brief glimpse of that time with No. 75029 passing Garth-y-dwr with the 16.15 Llangollen to Glyndyfrdwy train on 28 June 1993.

Crossing Dee Bridge with the 16.00 Llangollen to Glyndyfrdwy train is another ex-BR Standard 4MT, No. 80079, which is the tank version of resident locomotive No. 76079. No. 80079 had arrived from the Severn Valley Railway (SVR) just after having a general overhaul; indeed, SVR had not had time to line paint the locomotive before its visit to the railway. 2 July 1993.

With the visit of No. 80079, the opportunity was taken to renumber the locomotive to one its classmates – in this instance No. 80072, which was under restoration at the railway – to help the owning group receive some useful publicity. In this view No. 80072 is passing No. 13 signal on the approach to Glyndyfrdwy station with a mixed train comprising two Suburban passenger coaches and three goods vans on the summer evening of 17 July 1993.

Another view of temporary renumbered No. 80072, seen taking on water between service trains at Llangollen station on 13 August 1993. The locomotive has a '6D' shed plate on the smokebox door, which represents Shrewsbury steam shed during the 1960s. Alongside No. 80072 is a former LNER (Thompson) lounge buffet carriage, No. 1706, which was built in 1947 and had only been fully restored a few months previously.

Only a few months previously, Glyndyfrdwy Signal Box was painted in Great Western colours. Seen here now in London Midland maroon colours, former Great Western 2800 Class 2-8-0 locomotive No. 3822 arrives at the station with the 14.15 train from Llangollen. No. 3822 was built at Swindon in 1940 and was hired in from the Didcot Railway Centre. 6 September 1993.

Compare this image with the one taken in 1985 at the beginning of this book. On the face of it, not much has changed. However, appearances can deceive; various improvements had taken place, although they were not visible except for the introduction of signalling at the station. Taken from Castle Street bridge, this is the view on 9 October 1993, with No. 76079 having just arrived with its train from Glyndyfrdwy.

With the failure of *Flying Scotsman* twelve months previous, the railway was given the opportunity to hire in the locomotive once again, but this time in its ex-British Railways condition as No. 60103 complete with German-type smoke deflectors. On probably what could be the shortest goods train *Flying Scotsman* has hauled in its long history, it is seen passing Garth-y-dwr with the 10.20 train to Glyndyfrdwy on 26 March 1994 during a steam gala weekend.

Probably for the first time in preservation, ex-Southern West Country class locomotive No. 34027 *Taw Valley* hauls a goods/parcel train across Dee Bridge on a '8G Freight' private charter on 28 March 1994. To make No. 34027 feel at home, there were two former Southern bogie vans included in the eight-coach consist, which are immediately behind the locomotive.

Seen just after a spring snow flurry and creating an atmospheric departure from Berwyn station is No. 34027 *Taw Valley* on the final train of the day with the 17.15 Llangollen to Glyndyfrdwy train on 2 April 1994. *Taw Valley* had previously arrived from the North Yorkshire Moors Railway for a three-month loan period and it proved to be a popular visitor while at the railway.

Showing the British Railways lined Brunswick Green livery to very good effect, No. 60103 *Flying Scotsman* reverses back onto the Goods Yard line to the shed at Llangollen Goods Junction. The driver looking out of the cab window is Colin Dobson, while the fireman standing on the footplate is John Johnson. Both regular volunteers at the railway at the time, I am sure they felt privileged to have the opportunity to be on this famous locomotive.

Springtime in the Dee Valley is always a good time to visit the railway, and when you combined it with probably the most famous locomotive in the world, then you cannot go far wrong. Seen on the final approach to Glyndyfrdwy station, No. 60103 *Flying Scotsman* steams past with the 14.15 ex-Llangollen train. The sheep are oblivious to this event, with far important matters to attend to, it being lambing season! 10 April 1994.

Resplendent in Great Western livery, new restored Pannier tank No. 7754 departs Berwyn station with the 13.15 train to Glyndyfrdwy on 8 May 1994. No. 7754 was built by North British Locomotive Company (Glasgow) in 1930 and worked in a number of former Great Western locations until 1959, when it was sold to the National Coal Board, consequently working in various collieries in South Wales. In the mid-1970s it was finally withdrawn from traffic and donated to the National Museum of Wales, before it was permanently moved to the Llangollen Railway, where it was eventually restored to full working order.

Looking towards the hills of Bryn Newydd, departing from Deeside Halt with the 14.15 Llangollen to Glyndyfrdwy train is West Country class No. 34027 *Taw Valley*. Numerous locations near the lineside are not accessible unless there is a public footpath nearby. Access to this location, for example, was only possible due to the kind generosity of the farm owner, which was much appreciated. 8 May 1994.

Seen from the top of the signal at Llangollen Goods Junction on 26 June 1994, visiting Midland 4F 0-6-0 No. 44422 leads No. 34027 *Taw Valley* on the 'Pines Express', recreating a combination and train that used to operate on the Somerset & Dorset line during the 1950s and early '60s. The 4F was built in 1927 at Derby Works and was on hire from the North Staffordshire Railway (now the Churnet Valley Railway).

During the weekend of 11 and 12 June 1994, with
the visit of No. 34027 *Taw Valley* and 4F No. 44422
and resident locomotives Jinty No. 47298 and 4MT
No. 76079, the opportunity was taken to organise a
Somerset & Dorset Gala event as classmates of the
above locomotives were commonplace on this famous
line. Some location names on the railway were even
changed to represent those on the former S&D line.
In this view. No. 76079, renumbered 76029, departs the
east end of Coombe Down Tunnel (i.e. Berwyn Tunnel).

An opportunity presented itself during the S&D Gala weekend when three locomotives would all be in
view. No. 76029 (No 76079) has arrived at Llangollen Goods Junction to exchange the single line token
with the signalman before handing it over to the driver of 4F No. 44422 in order to take its train to
Glyndyfrdwy. Looking on, No. 34027 (as classmate No. 34045 *Ottery St Mary*) waits to travel light engine
to Llangollen station. Out of image was Jinty No. 47298, having being renumbered as No. 47275 for the
weekend. 12 June 1994.

Working away from Llangollen Goods Junction, Jinty No. 7298 – now in LMS black livery – attacks the climb towards Dee Bridge with its five-coach 16.00 passenger train to Glyndyfrdwy. The train is passing Pentrefelin Carriage Sidings, and just above is the footpath that runs alongside the Llangollen Canal. 2 April 1995.

An autumn view taken from the layby on the A5 London to Holyhead road overlooking Deeside Halt shows the scenic beauty of the line as it winds its way through the Dee Valley. Jinty No. 7298, now facing east, works away from the halt with the 13.38 Glyndyfrdwy to Llangollen train on 15 October 1995.

With the cold winter sun peeking through the surrounding mountains, Jinty No. 7298 and its lovely white exhaust are highlighted as it works away from Glyndyfrdwy station with the 12.47 'Santa' train to Llangollen. Leading up to Christmas, Glyndyfrdwy station is transformed into Santa's Grotto and is popular with children hoping to meet Father Christmas and his little helpers! 10 December 1995.

Although frowned upon by railway enthusiasts, most preserved railways would be poorer without the assistance of the Reverend Wilbert Awdry's *Thomas the Tank Engine* books and characters. Twice a year on the Llangollen Railway they hold Thomas and Friends special events where locomotives and staff become characters from the books, proving very popular with families. In this view, Jinty No. 7298 takes on the role of Thomas the Tank Engine, complete with face, as it departs from Glyndyfrdwy on 14 February 1996.

An image set up at Llangollen station with the assistance of some portable floodlights. Having just being repainted into British Railways plain black livery, Jinty No. 47298 stands ahead of a short goods train with Standard 4MT No. 76079 parked on the adjoining line to complete the picture. The significance of the image is that both locomotives were stablemates at Sutton Oak (8G) steam shed in St Helens during the late 1950s and early 1960s. 23 March 1996.

On loan from the Birmingham Railway Museum, Great Western Castle class No. 5080 *Defiant* approaches the Glyndyfrdwy distant signal at Garth-y-dwr while hauling the 'Berwyn Belle' dining train on 6 April 1996. The van immediately behind the locomotive was a former horse box, converted into a generator van to provide power for the dining train. Later on, this train formed the 14.00 'Wedding Belle' train for a wedding reception party.

Only a few days previously, the line to Carrog was officially opened and therefore Glyndyfrdwy station was now a passing station on the line. Arriving at the station on the down main (through) line, No. 7822 *Foxcote Manor* rolls pass the former station house, which is in private ownership, with 15.00 train to Carrog on 12 May 1996.

A locomotive that became very popular on its summer visit to the railway was ex-BR(W) 0-4-2T Collett 1400 class No. 1450, seen passing a nice bank of bluebells after crossing the Dee Bridge with the 16.25 Llangollen to Carrog goods train during the late Spring Gala weekend event. No. 1450 was owned by Mike Little and was normally at the South Devon Railway. 27 May 1996.

When the news arrived that No. 1450 was to visit the railway, the author approached Chief Mechanical Engineer Dave Owens, asking whether it would also be possible to hire in South Devon Railways ex-BR(W) auto-coach W228W as both the carriage and the locomotive class were once an everyday occurrence on former Great Western branch lines. The plan was agreed with, provided the cost of transporting W228W to and from Llangollen was not paid for by the railway. In consequence, a number of private charters operated on the railway to cover this cost and this classic combination is seen passing Berwyn station on one of those charters on 8 June 1996.

Just west of Glyndyfrdwy station the line runs alongside the River Dee, and accessing this location only became possible due to a number of railway volunteers and photographers who cleared the various bushes and trees that were obscuring the line from the opposite side of the river. Their efforts were rewarded as, on the same summer sunny evening as the previous image, No. 1450 and auto-coach W228W roll past on their way to Carrog.

At the same time that 0-4-2T No. 1450 arrived at Llangollen, ex-BR(W) small Prairie 2-6-2T No. 5541 was loaned from the Dean Forest Railway for a short period to work some of the railway's passenger trains in the early summer. Seen moving away from Llangollen Goods Junction, No. 5541 works its typical branch line train with the 17.00 train to Carrog during the late afternoon of 27 May 1996.

Ex-BR(W) Small Prairie 2-6-2T No. 5541 passes the Glyndyfrdwy outer starter signal with the 14.20 Llangollen to Carrog train on 12 June 1996. Photographing from this location was only possible during the early summer when the sun was high enough and far enough around in the sky to light up the area, including the River Dee, which runs alongside the line at this particular point.

Hauling two ex-British Railways Mk 1 Suburban coaches and two four-wheel box vans, recreating a typical branch train of yesteryear, Small Prairie No. 5541 passes Garth-y-dwr with a private photographic charter on the nice summer's evening of 12 June 1996.

Ex-BR(W) 0-4-2T 1400 Class No. 1450 with auto-coach W228 passes Garth-y-dwr on another private photographic charter on the evening of the longest day of the year, 21 June 1996. No. 1450 was designed by C. B. Collett, CME of the Great Western Railway, and was built at Swindon works in 1935. The class was paired with auto-coaches in a push/pull formation to work branch line trains. The auto-coaches were fitted with apparatus to allow the driver of the locomotive to work the train when going backwards without the need of the locomotive to run round its coach.

Taken with a telephoto lens and looking up the River Dee, 0-4-2T No. 1450 (renumbered as 'local' 84J Croes Newydd locomotive No. 1416) and auto-coach W228 head to Carrog on the same summer evening as the previous image. The location was near to the Fisherman's Crossing, just half a mile west of Glyndyfrdwy station.

Another image of this classic combination of No. 1450 and auto-coach W228, this time taken mid-morning as the train approaches No. 2 home signal for Glyndyfrdwy station on 22 June 1996. In the background is the River Dee as it winds its way through the scenic valley. The road bridge that crosses the river at this point provides a scenic back route from Glyndyfrdwy to Carrog and ultimately to Berwyn.

After departing from Glyndyfrdwy station on 13 July 1996, No. 1450 and auto-coach W228W catch the golden rays of the setting sun on another private charter. This private charter and the others that were arranged during this period paid for the transportation of the auto-coach to and from the South Devon Railway but also allowed the general public an opportunity to ride on this combination in normal operation.

No. 1450 and auto-coach W228 are seen upon arrival at Carrog station just after sunset. With the assistance of a couple of portable floodlights, and with the station and signal box lights on, an atmospheric scene is created at this beautiful country station. The line from Glyndyfrdwy to Carrog was officially opened two months previously on 2 May. The restoration of Carrog was carried out by a group called the 'Friends of Carrog', who did an excellent job. 13 July 1996.

Framed by tree branches, BR Standard 4MT No. 76079 works away from Carrog with a fourteen-vehicle goods train heading to Glyndyfrdwy on the nice autumn morning of 5 November 1996. Preserved railways are treated as tourist attractions, meaning they rely on the public to visit and ride on the trains. However, the railways are also preserving our history too, which includes the preservation of goods wagons among other things. Although they do not earn any income, they are still an important part of our history for the public to appreciate and act as a reminder of the past.

Passing Hendom on the Carrog and Glyndyfrdwy section of the line, the beautiful autumn tints are shown to good effect as BR Standard 4MT No. 76079 with its mixed goods train heads towards the next station on the line: Glyndyfrdwy. This section of line is an excellent advert for the railway as it runs alongside the A5 Holyhead to London road. People in passing cars cannot help but look at the marvel of a steam train passing through beautiful countryside. 5 November 1996.

As well as carrying people, the railways were also important in the transportation of goods, and this included other forms of transport too. In this image, Jinty No. 47298 is seen at Carrog station while waiting to depart with a demonstration War Department train comprising three army vehicles on flat wagons as part of a War Gala weekend event. 4 August 1996.

Shorter daylight hours and the lower sun during the winter months sometimes create 'atmospheric' images of steam locomotives at work. After departing Llangollen station with the 12.00 'Santa' train to Carrog, newly restored LMS Black 5 No. 4806 works hard as it approaches Llangollen Goods Junction Signal Box. With the sun partly hidden by a tree branch, the backlight provides a silhouette effect on the locomotive and the resulting steam exhaust. 22 December 1996.

Taken from Inman's Woods, high above Llangollen, and looking down towards Pentrefelin Sidings, BR Manor Class No. 7822 *Foxcote Manor* and its six coaches start the climb to Dee Bridge and Berwyn with the 13.00 Llangollen to Carrog 'Santa' train. 22 December 1996.

The best time to photograph steam locomotives is the winter, not just for the cold temperatures which assist in producing good steam exhausts, but for the low winter sun light too. Having arrived at the railway only a few days previously, ex-BR(W) Pannier 0-6-0PT No. 9681 is seen passing Hendom on 5 January 1997 with the 13.00 Llangollen to Carrog train.

On a crisp winter's day, and providing a lovely trailing steam exhaust, former GWR Pannier 0-6-0PT No. 9681 and two ex-BR Suburban coaches cross the River Dee at Pentrefelin with the 11.00 train to Carrog. No. 9681 had arrived from the Dean Forest Railway for a three-month loan period to cover the off-peak passenger service, as unfortunately the railway's own Pannier, No. 7754, was undergoing boiler repairs at the time. 25 January 1997.

No. 9681 passes Hendom on a return late afternoon train from Carrog, with Glyndyfrdwy being the next stop on its way to Llangollen. No. 9681 was built by British Railways Swindon Works in 1949 and spent its life in South Wales before withdrawal in July 1965. It then languished in a breaker's yard before being rescued for restoration ten years later. 25 January 1997.

In a tranquil scene taken on the late afternoon of 25 January 1997, No. 9681 is seen resting at Llangollen station after the final passenger train of the day had operated. The locomotive departed shortly afterwards to the shed yard to be watered and coaled in readiness for the following day's passenger service.

The railway's own Pannier, No. 7754, which had been under repairs for several months, returned to service just in time for a number of private charters. Seen here just after arrival at Glyndyfrdwy, the locomotive – looking resplendent in ex-works condition – heads a goods train which was typical of the period during the 1950s. The locomotive was about to take water before proceeding to Carrog. 17 March 1997.

An image taken in dramatic lighting conditions, Nos 9681 and 7754 double-head a long goods train as it approaches Pearson's Farm at Garth-y-dwr on 13 March 1997. Both locomotives on this particular occasion were renumbered to represent two ex-84J Croes Newydd (Wrexham) steam shed locomotives, being No. 4645 and No. 8727 respectively during the late 1950s. It is very possible the real Nos 4645 and 8727 locomotives had visited Llangollen during their late British Railway lives, hence taking their identities.

The following day, both locomotives reverted to their own identities. In more dramatic lighting conditions, No. 9681 heads the goods train with No. 7754 providing banking assistance at the rear as the train passes Fisherman's Crossing just west of Glyndyfrdwy. 14 March 1997.

Another visitor to the railway – and a first for the line even in British Railways days – ex-LMS Jubilee Class No. 45593 *Kolhapur* in BR lined Brunswick Green with a rake of chocolate and cream coaches passes Fisherman's Crossing on the 13.00 Llangollen to Carrog train. The locomotive was built by the LMS at Crewe Works in 1936 and was on loan from the Birmingham Railway Museum. 29 March 1997.

Having recently been returned to working order, ex-LMS Black 5 No. 4806 approaches Garth-y-dwr with the 12.00 train to Carrog on 31 March 1997. No. 4806 was withdrawn by British Railways in 1968 and was purchased by the late Kenneth Aldcroft for further use in north-west England. Eventually the locomotive arrived at the heritage railway in 1993, where it was subjected to a major overhaul, returning to steam in late 1996.

Visiting the railway during the summer of 1997 was former BR Class 1F 0-6-0T No. 41708, seen here with a short mixed parcels/passenger train and passing Garth-y-dwr on the lovely spring evening of 24 May 1997. The first vehicle behind the locomotive is a former LMS 50-foot Braked Parcels Coach, which had only been restored to running order a few months previously.

Now seen on a short goods train, half-cab No. 41708 is working hard from Carrog station on the early summer morning of 19 July 1997. No. 47108 was built in Derby 1880 to a Johnson Midland Railway design and was finally withdrawn in 1966. These locos had the nickname of 'half-cabs' due to having a short cab roof, with the rear open to the elements.

Another visitor to the railway in the summer of 1997 was another 100+-year-old locomotive – former London North Western Railway Coal Tank 0-6-2T No. 1054, which was on loan from the Keighley & Worth Valley Railway. No. 1054 was built at Crewe Works in 1888 to a Francis Webb design and was finally withdrawn by British Railways as No. 58926 in 1958. In this view, the locomotive is working a short passenger train on the approach to Carrog station during the sunny late spring morning of 31 May 1997.

Another view of Coal Tank No. 1054, on this occasion hauling a short parcels train and having a short break at Deeside Signal Box on 10 June 1997. The signal box, based on a London Midland design, was built and opened in 1990 to control the trains initially arriving at the halt when it acted as a terminus. It eventually became a passing loop for trains to and from Glyndyfrdwy.

Leading Standard 4MT No. 76079, Jinty No. 47298 works away from Carrog with a late afternoon train to Llangollen during the annual 'Transport Extravaganza' weekend event. By coincidence, both locomotives were owned by Derek Foster, who was also a driver at the railway; in this instance, he was driving No. 76079. The blue coach in the train's formation was part of the line's 'Berwyn Belle' dining train. 14 September 1997.

Arriving at the railway just before the start of the 'Santa' trains was David Shepherd's Class 9F 2-10-0 No. 92203 *Black Prince*, which was normally based at the East Somerset Railway. In low winter sunlight, No. 92203 is seen here approaching Dee Bridge, Pentrefelin, with the 12.00 'Santa' train to Carrog on 20 December 1997. Providing assistance at the rear of the train is Pannier No. 7754, although in theory it was not required as the 9F is more than capable of hauling this train on its own.

Now minus its nameplates, 9F No. 92203 *Black Prince* with ten maroon BR Mk 1 coaches in tow approaches Glyndyfrdwy outer home No. 2 signal with a private charter on 19 March 1998. No. 92203 was built in 1959 at Swindon Works and had a working career of less than nine years, having been withdrawn by British Railways in November 1967, when David Shepherd purchased the locomotive for the princely sum of £3,000.

Working past Fisherman's Crossing in excellent lighting conditions, No. 92203 shows what it is capable of in hauling its private charter train. The charter recreated a former Somerset & Dorset passenger service train from July 1960, with No. 92203 working 'M227', the 09.35 SO Nottingham to Bournemouth train, over the line. Completing the scene, the loco displayed the unique S&D express lamp headcode complete with 82F Bath Green Park shedcode plate. 19 March 1998.

Daffodils in bloom mean only one thing: the Dee Valley wakes up to springtime not only with the birds singing, trees coming alive and newborn lambs, but also to the sound and beat of 9F No. 92203 as it works its ten-coach train the last few yards towards Carrog station. In the foreground is one of the restored station lamps that overlook the footpath entrance to Platform 2 and the restored waiting room. 19 March 1998.

A scene that could almost be reminiscent of the Somerset & Dorset line as 9F No. 92203 storms out of Coombe Down Tunnel on a train to Bournemouth in 1960. In reality, the locomotive is storming out of the west end of the 689-yard Berwyn Tunnel on 19 March 1998.

In photography, the period of daytime shortly after sunrise or before sunset, during which daylight is softer and redder, is often called the golden hour. In this instance, an opportunity arose to take advantage of this light, and approaching Hendom, midway between Carrog and Glyndyfrdwy, 9F No. 92203 and train lap up the golden rays of the setting sun on the final working of the day. 19 March 1998.

Seen from high on the slope of Pen-y-Garth, Pannier No. 7754 with its two Suburban coaches ambles along on the 11.00 Llangollen to Corwen train as it passes Pearson's Farm on the approach to Garth-y-dwr. 22 March 1998.

Standing within a few yards of the previous image and framed in the trees, Pannier No. 7754 continues to amble along with the 11.00 train to Carrog as it approaches the distant signal for Glyndyfrdwy at Garth-y-dwr. 22 March 1998.

On a clear sunny day and with the peaks of Moel Morfydd, Moel-y-Gamelin and Moel-y-Faen (Llantysilio Mountain) in the background, Pannier No. 7754 works bunker-first with the return 11.50 Carrog to Llangollen train on the approach to Berwyn Tunnel. The image is taken from a layby on the A5 Holyhead to London road, which overlooks Deeside Halt. 22 March 1998.

You would be forgiven if you thought this was taken in the winter, yet it was taken mid-April after some unusual arctic weather had hit the United Kingdom. With the kind permission of the local farmer to access this location, seen from the lower slopes of Moel Fferna at Carrog-Isaf, BR 9F No. 92203 *Black Prince* passes Hendom with the 14.00 train to Carrog on 12 April 1998.

During special event weekends on the railway, the opportunity is taken to double-head some passenger trains during the course of the weekend. On the occasion of the 50 Years of British Railways Gala, the railway paired BR 4MT No. 76079 and BR Black 5 No. 44806 together for the 11.00 train to Carrog. They are seen here departing in a cloud of steam at Llangollen station on 25 May 1998.

Admiring ex-BR Large Prairie 2-6-2T No. 4141 working its goods train up Berwyn Bank, the railway's Chief Mechanical Engineer, Dave Owen, is waiting for the train to arrive at the station to take over driving the locomotive for the remainder of the journey to Carrog on 12 June 1998.

On a clear early summer evening, BR Large Prairie No. 4141 approaches Deeside Halt with its thirteen-wagon goods train on 12 June 1998. No. 4141 was built at Swindon Works in 1946, being based at Gloucester Horton Road steam shed (85B) before being withdrawn by British Railways in March 1963. It was then sold to Woodham Bros in Barry, South Wales, before being purchased for restoration in 1973. It took another twenty-five years before it was finally returned to steam.

Approaching the distant signal for Glyndyfrdwy at Garth-y-dwr, Large Prairie No. 4141 rounds the curve with a private charter goods train on 12 June 1998. The location of this signal was decided by the author and friend Brian Dobbs with assistance from John d'E. Stowell, who was the railway's Signal & Telegraph Engineer in the early 1990s. The distant signal arm is of North Eastern origin, rather than the expected Great Western origin, which would be more in keeping with the line.

Seen from the north side of the River Dee, and with its goods train in tow, Large Prairie No. 4141 heads into the sun as it travels west to Carrog after leaving Glyndyfrdwy station. The building highlighted on the hill is the Berwyn Arms Hotel, which is on the A5 London to Holyhead road. 12 June 1998.

In ideal conditions, with hard frost on the ground on a December morning, the front of Black 5 No. 44806 is highlighted by leaking steam leaving a lovely trailing exhaust as it passes Hendom with the 11.00 Llangollen to Carrog 'Santa' train on 20 December 1998.

Framed by the arch of the B5437 bridge, Large Prairie No. 4141 sits quietly at Carrog station with its goods train while the locomotive crew have a deserved break in the station. It is hard to believe from this image that the station was previously closed and left to nature, but due to the 'Friends of Carrog' the station has been beautifully restored back to its former glory. 3 March 1999.

Lit by the low setting sun with the backdrop of the B5437 road bridge, Large Prairie No. 4141 has just arrived with its three Suburban coaches at Carrog station on 3 March 1999. Behind the train, through the arch, is the recently restored signal box at the station.

During the course of a mini winter event weekend, Jinty No. 47298 approaches Owain Glyndwr's Mound with the 12.38 Llangollen to Carrog goods train on 7 February 1999. This location is named after Owain Glyndwr, who resided at Glyndyfrdwy and was the self-proclaimed Prince of Wales during the early fifteenth century when Wales was seeking independence from English rule.

Spring is in the air and Black 5 No. 44806 hauls a fourteen-wagon goods train on a private charter on 31 March 1999 as it approaches Owain Glyndwr's Mound, just west of Hendom on the Glyndyfrdwy to Carrog section of the line. The mound – the remains of a twelfth-century castle motte – occupies a commanding position over the Dee Valley and is visible from the nearby A5 road.

Seen from the public footpath that originates from the nearby A5 road – which goes under the railway at this point, then heads to the River Dee – Large Prairie No. 4141 approaches Deeside Halt with its mixed goods train from Llangollen to Carrog on 14 April 1999.

With a foreboding cloud in the background, Large Prairie No. 4141 puts out a good steam exhaust on its typical branch line passenger train consisting of three Suburban coaches as it passes Fisherman's Crossing, Glyndyfrdwy, on 14 April 1999. The train is heading to Carrog station, where it will have a short break before returning bunker-first to Llangollen station.

Seen here at Tanners Reach, near Berwyn Tunnel, Great Western 5600 Class 0-6-2T No. 5637 works through the spring valley of trees as it heads to Deeside Halt on 20 May 1999. The locomotive was designed by C. B. Collett and was built at the Great Western Swindon Works in 1925, working mainly in the South Wales valleys. No. 5637 was eventually withdrawn by British Railways in 1964 before eventual purchase from Woodham Bros, Barry, ten years later. It took another twenty-four years before it worked its first train.

On hire from the Swindon & Cricklade Railway, 0-6-2T No. 5637 approaches Deeside Halt Signal Box on a misty mid-spring morning with its three-coach train. Deeside Halt is only open during a high-intensity timetable service, such as gala events where there are two or more trains operating on the line. Otherwise it remains just a request station halt and passing point for trains between Berwyn and Glyndyfrdwy. 20 May 1999.

In apparently Great Western 'green' livery, No. 5637 and three coaches depart Llangollen station with an evening private photographic charter to Carrog. On its way No. 5637 will perform a number of staged run pasts for the benefit of a group of photographers in glorious evening springtime light. 20 May 1999.

This is one of the author's favourite images taken at the railway, with the driver, Aled Roberts, posing for the camera while on the footplate of a gleaming Manor class locomotive, No. 7822 *Foxcote Manor,* which had been recommissioned the day after its second general overhaul. Aled Roberts was a popular character on the railway, and he could tell you a few stories about his career. 29 August 1999.

Photographed from the A5 road on a nice autumn day, Large Prairie No. 4141 approaches Owain Glyndwr's Mound with the 13.00 Llangollen to Carrog train during the *Thomas the Tank Engine* weekend event on 31 October 1999. The reason for the side-on shot was to avoid seeing the 'face' on the front of the locomotive during these particular events.

Taken with a short telephoto lens, No. 7822 *Foxcote Manor* works rounds the curve at Garth-y-dwr with its passenger train as the autumn colours begin to show in the Dee Valley on 2 November 1999. The yellow object in the image is a milepost; these are a common occurrence on railway lines (as well as roads) and this one represents a distance of 10 miles from Ruabon where the line began prior to the mid-1960s.

A shaft of winter sunlight lights up ex-Great Western 4200 Class 2-8-0T No. 4277, which leaves a trail of steam exhaust in the Dee Valley as it tows its seven coaches on 19 December 1999. Taken from the mound at Hendom, No. 4277 is forming the 11.00 Llangollen to Carrog 'Santa' train. It arrived at the railway from the North Yorkshire Moors Railway for a four-month loan period.

Visiting from the South Devon Railway, 2251 Class 0-6-0 No. 3205 is seen double-heading with Manor Class No. 7822 *Foxcote Manor* while recreating a scene from 1961, complete with nine coaches and a 'Cambrian Coast Express' (CCE) headboard, as it passes Garth-y-dwr on 13 March 2000. The original 'CCE' ran from London to Shrewsbury then on to Aberystwyth and Pwllheli. The train was double-headed from Shrewsbury, usually hauled by Manor and Dukedog class locomotives, although occasionally a 2251 Class locomotive was used.

With the assistance of some portable floodlights and looking from the waiting room, Nos 3205 and 7822 *Foxcote Manor* are lit up nicely while waiting to depart Llangollen station with the 'Cambrian Coast Express' on the evening of 13 March 2000.

Llangollen station has a prominent location within the town, especially as it is located on the banks of the River Dee, and therefore it is unlikely you would miss the station buildings and distinctive covered footbridge while walking around the town. Photographed from Platform 2, 0-6-0 No. 3205 poses with its thirteen-wagon goods train, while the crew take a break before their eventual departure to Carrog. 4 April 2000.

Seen on 4 April 2000, another view of this classic and well-known location on the line is Berwyn station, Berwyn Viaduct and the Chain Bridge over the River Dee, enhanced by the snow on the Berwyn Hills in the background. This time Collett-designed 0-6-0 No. 3205 departs from the station with its goods train to Carrog. No. 3205 was built at Swindon Works in 1946 and was withdrawn by British Railways in 1965, being the only member of a class of 120 locomotives that survived into preservation.

Taken from the public footpath that runs through Pearson's Farm at Garth-y-dwr, and in the shadow of Pen-y-Garth, 2-8-0T No. 4277, now resplendent in British Railways plain black livery, heads to Glyndyfrdwy with its goods train on 5 April 2000. No. 4277 was built by Great Western in 1920 at Swindon Works and was used mainly on short-haul coal trains in the Welsh Valleys. It was withdrawn by British Railways in 1964 before being purchased from Woodham Bros, Barry, in 1986 for eventual restoration.

Above and below: Two images taken within a few seconds of each other but showing the beauty of the line as it wanders through the Dee Valley on 5 April 2000. The first image, taken from the public footpath that goes around Pen-y-Garth, sees No. 4277 and its train pass the 1,000-yard gate (the distance from Deeside Halt), with Bryn Dol Fawr in the background. In the second image, a panoramic view of the partial snow-covered slopes of Graig-Ddu and Moel Morfydd gives a good view of the rear of the train as it heads to Garth-y-dwr and onward to Glyndyfrdwy.

Approaching Glyndyfrdwy west distant signal is 2-8-0 No. 5197, a United States Army Transportation Corps Class S160, designed for use in Europe during the Second World War. This particular locomotive was built by Lima Locomotive Works (Ohio) in 1945 and spend most of its working life in China until the early 1990s. In 1995, Derek Foster purchased No. 5197, restoring and returning the locomotive to traffic in 1998. No. 5197 is seen here working the 14.25 Carrog to Llangollen train on 30 April 2000.

With the banks of the River Dee overflowing near Pentrefelin, Pannier No. 7754 works its short ballast train across Dee Bridge on 31 October 2000. It was unusual to see the River Dee so high, but after a recent bout of heavy rain, the resulting water had to go somewhere.

Passing Garth-y-dwr on a lovely autumn day is a rare sight of an engineers' ballast train consisting of three Catfish ballast wagons, one Dogfish ballast wagon and a Shark van being hauled by Pannier No. 7754, all by coincidence in matching black livery. You will note the vehicles have marine-sounding names, which was normal practice when working for British Railways. The Shark van has mini ploughs attached; as the ballast is dropped from the wagons, the ploughs spread the ballast evenly across the track. 31 October 2000.

In dramatic weather conditions, just after a heavy rain shower, a rainbow appears as the sun lights up Jinty No. 47298, looking a bit work-stained while hauling its two coaches past Garth-y-dwr on a Llangollen to Carrog private charter train. 16 March 2001.

Looking better for its work-stained 1950s appearance, Jinty No. 47298 works past Garth-y-dwr on a short goods train to Carrog on the afternoon of 16 March 2001. Garth-y-dwr has always been popular for photographers, being surrounded by the lush hills, and with the line at this point on a gentle incline, you are always guaranteed to get some steam exhaust from the passing locomotives.

Resplendent in British Railways post-1959 lined livery, Black 5 No. 44806 rounds the curve at Garth-y-dwr with its five chocolate and cream coaches forming the 11.00 Llangollen to Carrog train on the beautiful spring day of 7 April 2002. The Black 5 is showing an 8C Speke Junction steam shed-plate, where it was allocated for a brief time in the mid-1960s before withdrawal in 1968.

In a scene that could have been from the late 1950s, when the line was opened between Dolgellau and Ruabon, No. 7822 *Foxcote Manor* hauls its goods train under the B5437 road bridge, passing the beautiful restored Carrog station before heading on to Llangollen and Ruabon (well, wishful thinking, but a nice thought). This view certainly shows the station at its best, with the lovely gardens, milk churns, porter's barrow and station lamps all adding to the ambience. 11 April 2002.

Passing Owain Glyndwr's Mound, and now facing east, No. 7822 *Foxcote Manor* produces lively steam exhaust as it heads to Llangollen on 11 April 2002. Occasionally when a resident locomotive leaves the line to visit another railway, upon its return the opportunity is sometimes taken to have the locomotive facing the opposite direction, especially as the railway does not have a turntable to carry out such a manoeuvre.

Departing from Glyndyfrdwy station, and about to pass the signal box, the fireman of No. 7822 *Foxcote Manor* is about to hand the single line token to the signalman, which will allow the goods train to travel in safety onto the Glyndyfrdwy to Llangollen Goods Junction single line. On the left is the apparatus which allows for the collection and setting down of Royal Mail postal bags without the train needing to stop. 11 April 2002.

Waiting to depart from Carrog station is *Foxcote Manor*, albeit in the disguise of one of its long-gone classmates, No. 7800 *Torquay Manor*, complete with a 'Cambrian Coast Express' headboard and a typical early 1960s coach formation. Alongside the train is the excellently rebuilt Carrog Signal Box, which adds more character to the whole station. 29 April 2002.

A view taken from the A5 road by the Berwyn Arms, and looking west down the Dee Valley towards Carrog, No. 7800 *Torquay Manor* and its eight-coach train approach the distant signal for Glyndyfrdwy station. The train was a recreation of a typical 'Cambrian Coast Express' service complete with headboard and running in coach boards too. 29 April 2002.

The following day, *Foxcote Manor* kept the identity of classmate No. 7800 *Torquay Manor* and subsequently worked a fourteen-wagon goods train typical of the late 1950s and early 1960s. While the sheep in the foreground seem to be oblivious to the main attraction, the train is seen passing Hendom on its way to Llangollen on 30 April 2002.

Carrying on with the theme of changing identities, No. 7822 *Foxcote Manor* now appears as No. 7817 *Garsington Manor* and is seen arriving at Glyndyfrdwy station with the 19.15 Llangollen to Carrog private charter organised by the Foxcote Manor Society on 20 June 2002. No. 7822 also appeared as No. 7807 *Compton Manor* earlier in the month as a surprise for one of their members, Mick Compton.

It is autumn again, which provides colour but also varied weather conditions too. The day of this train, the weather threw everything at the photographer, from heavy rain to crisp sunshine and everything in between. With a lucky break in the clouds, and dominated by the foreground tree, the sun appears as Pannier No. 7754 and two Suburban coaches approach Hendom on 10 November 2002.

Taken from the lower slopes of Moel Fferna at Carrog-Isaf, overlooking Owain Glyndwr's Mound on the left, Pannier No. 7754 is steaming well as it passes by with a short passenger train from Carrog to Llangollen on the afternoon of 10 November 2002.

A new addition to the railway was former Great Western 2-6-2T No. 5199, which had only returned to steam a few weeks previously after an eighteen-year restoration to working order. The locomotive is approaching Llangollen Goods Junction with the 10.30 Llangollen to Carrog train, consisting of three Suburban coaches and a four-wheel van, on 13 April 2003. No. 5199 was built at Swindon Works in 1934 and spent most of its life in the Midlands before being withdrawn in 1963. It then languished at Woodham Bros for twenty-two years before being purchased by the Great Western Steam Locomotive Group.

The railway's resident Pannier, No. 7754, was hired for the day by a group of railway photographers, taking the opportunity to photograph the locomotive and its goods train at various locations along the line, including places that were not regularly photographed on normal timetable days. The following four images are a small selection from what was obtained. With No. 7754 now facing east, she is seen producing a smoke ring from her chimney as she passes Owain Glyndwr's Mound. 19 March 2003.

Working gently into Glyndyfrdwy station, No. 7754 and train pass the former Barmouth South Signal Box, located at the west end of the station. It is a Grade II listed building and because it could not remain in position for operational reasons at Barmouth, it was moved and rebuilt at Glyndyfrdwy in 1999 as a non-operational signal box. The image was taken from the former footbridge, which was dismantled a few years later due to ongoing corrosion. 19 March 2003.

Taken from inside Llangollen Goods Junction Signal Box, this is the view that the signalman has when a train arrives from Berwyn. No. 7754 passes with its ten-wagon goods train on the late afternoon of 19 March 2003 as it heads for the final half a mile to Llangollen station.

Another view taken at Llangollen Goods Junction, this time from the east end, showing the signal box, Great Western signals and the signal box lamp post as No. 7754 works gently away with its train. The line on the right-hand side is the access line to the locomotive/goods yard, as well as the carriage siding that runs alongside the main operating line into Llangollen station. 19 March 2003.

In British Railways plain black livery, 2-6-2T No. 5199 arrives at Deeside Halt with a midday Llangollen to Carrog train during a Spring Gala event weekend, while the signalman waits to receive the single line token. This view shows Deeside Halt to good effect, with the signal box, platform, GWR pagoda shelter and station sign on 13 April 2003.

The daffodils are in full bloom on the platform of Deeside Halt while Pannier No. 7754 sits bunker-first with its short ballast train on the passing loop. No. 7754 was waiting for a train from Carrog to pass before it proceeded forward to Glyndyfrdwy. 13 April 2003.

In September 2002, the railway was hired by a TV company to re-enact the famous Rainhill Trials of 1829 featuring the working replica locomotives of *Rocket*, *San Pareil* and *Novelty* to test the theory that *Rocket* won the trials on merit. The locomotives were on hire from the National Railway Museum, where they normally reside on display. The filming took place at Carrog station and in this view all three locomotives are seen together in steam in between trial workings. This provided useful publicity for the railway as the programme *Timewatch – Rocket and Its Rivals* was aired on BBC 2 in January 2003.

Hauling two replica Liverpool & Manchester Railway open coaches, *Rocket* – driven by Ray Trowell of the National Railway Museum – slowly approaches Carrog station on the sunny afternoon of Sunday 29 September 2002. Also in attendance was a replica of the fourth trial entry, the single-horse-powered *Cyclops*, which never stood a chance.

Former British Rail (BR) Class 03 shunter No. 03162 (D2162) is seen reversing a rake of stock into the former Pentrefelin Carriage Sidings on 1 November 1992. No. 03162 was built at Swindon Works in 1960 as D2162 and spent most of its life in Yorkshire and East Anglia before ending its career in Birkenhead in the late 1980s. Withdrawn in 1989, it was presented to Wirral Borough Council, who then loaned the shunter to the railway.

With Llangollen Goods Junction in the background and passing the carriage siding, ex-Class 25 Bo-Bo locomotive D7629 appearing in early British Railways two-tone green livery approaches Llangollen station with the 09.50 ex-Glyndyfrdwy train on 26 June 1993. D7629 was built by Beyer-Peacock in 1965 for British Rail(ways). Renumbered to 25279 in 1973, she was finally withdrawn in 1987 before being purchased by Martin Bell and operating on the railway until 1997.

Seen during the annual 'Transport Extravaganza' weekend event, ex-BR Class 24 No. 24081 is shunting some freight stock at Llangollen Goods Junction on 18 September 1993. No. 24081 began life as D5081, having been built at Crewe Works in 1960, and was renumbered to 24081 before eventual withdrawal in 1980. She was the last Class 24 to work for British Rail, and afterwards she was preserved at Steamport in Southport before arriving at the heritage railway.

Recreating a scene that was once commonplace on British Rail, two Class 25 locomotives are on the 'Cambrian Coast Express' to Pwllheli. Arriving at Llangollen station is No. 25313 with D7629 (No. 25279) on the ex-15.05 Glyndyfrdwy train during a Diesel Gala weekend event on 23 October 1993. No. 25313 was built at Derby Works in 1966, before being withdrawn in 1987 and purchased by Martin Bell. She arrived at the Llangollen Railway in 1988, lasting until 2009.

From the public footpath at Pearson's Farm, Garth-y-dwr, the railway's three resident diesel railcars are seen together passing with the 13.25 Glyndyfrdwy to Llangollen train on 21 May 1995. It is led by former British Rail Class 104 unit No. 50454/50528, Class 105 127 hybrid unit No. 56456/51618 and Class 108 unit No. 51907/54490; these railcars were withdrawn in 1993, 1983 and 1993 respectively before arriving at the railway, where they have proved popular with passengers due to the forward-facing views they provide.

With former BR Class 20 No. 20142 leading Class 25 No. 25313 in former British Rail blue livery, the pair approach Llangollen Goods Junction with the 17.00 Glyndyfrdwy to Llangollen train on 21 May 1995. No. 20142 was built in 1966 at the Vulcan Foundry as D8142 for British Railways, then became number 20142 in 1973 before being withdrawn twenty years later in 1993. She arrived at the railway in 1994 and remained until 1999. Turning full circle, No. 20142 is now back on the main line as part of the GBRf working fleet of locomotives.

Arriving at Llangollen station with a short goods train from the shed yard in mid-1950s British Railways livery is ex-BR Class 08 diesel shunter D3295 on 16 September 1995. These shunters were commonplace on British Rail, with over 900 being built between 1952 and 1962. D3265 (13265) was built at Derby in 1956, was renumbered to 08195 in 1973 and was withdrawn from Birkenhead in 1983.

Visiting the railway on 21 October 1995 was former BR diesel-hydraulic Warship D821 *Greyhound*. In glorious autumn sunlight, it is seen passing Garth-y-dwr on the 11.00 Llangollen to Glyndyfrdwy train, complete with 'The Royal Duchy' headboard. D821 was built at Swindon Works in 1960 and withdrawn in December 1972. Part of a class of thirty-eight, the Warships mainly worked trains between London and the West Country. The locomotive was then purchased by the Diesel Traction Group in May 1973, who have maintained it ever since.

A most unlikely visitor to the railway came in 1996 when ex-BR Deltic Class 55 No. 55015 *Tulyar* appeared for a three-month spell to work some of the timetable trains. The Deltics were better known for racing up and down the East Coast Main Line on ex-London King's Cross trains rather than working on a single branch line train in the Dee Valley! No. 55015, built in 1961 at the Vulcan Works and withdrawn by BR on 2 January 1992, is seen putting on the power as it passes Fisherman's Crossing with the 14.00 train to Carrog on 15 September 1996.

Now appearing in British Railways green livery, Class 20 D8142 approaches Glyndyfrdwy west distant signal with the 12.50 Carrog to Llangollen train on 20 October 1996 during a Diesel Gala weekend event.

With the driver peeking out of his cab, ex-BR Type 3 D6514 crosses Dee Bridge with the 17.00 Llangollen to Carrog train on 16 August 1997. This former British Rail locomotive arrived at the railway for a short loan period and was built by the Birmingham Railway Carriage & Wagon Company in 1960. In late 1973 it was reclassified as a Class 33 locomotive and renumbered as 33103 before being withdrawn in 1994. In 2002 it temporary returned to the main line after purchase by Fragonset Railways.

Approaching Hendom is former BR locomotive No. 47449. Wearing large logo blue livery, it is seen working a late afternoon Llangollen to Carrog train during the Transport Extravaganza weekend. This Type 4 locomotive was built at Crewe Works in 1964 as D1566. Renumbered 47449 in 1973, it was withdrawn from BR service in November 1993.

On hire from the Bo'ness & Kinneil Railway, ex-BR Class 26 No. 26004 awaits its next turn of duty in the sidings at Carrog station on 18 April 1998. No. 26004 was built as D5304 in 1958 by the Birmingham Railway Carriage & Wagon Company, before being renumbered 26004 in late 1973 and withdrawn in late 1992. The locomotive spent most of its life in Scotland and it is adorned in Railfreight coal sector livery.

Had the line remained open in the late 1960s and 1970s, this may have been the type of train operated on the line, headed by a Class 25 locomotive. In this instance, No. 25313 is seen passing Carrog Signal Box with the ex-16.00 train from Llangollen. By the time of this image was taken, on 18 April 1998, the locomotive had been named by the National Trust as *Chirk Castle/Castell y Waun*, which is a Grade I listed 700-year-old fortress guarding the Ceiriog Valley.

Another view of former BR Class 25 No. 25313 *Chirk Castle/Castell y Waun,* on this occasion heading east pass Garth-y-dwr with the 10.50 Carrog to Llangollen train during the railway's Transport Extravaganza weekend. No. 25313 is seen fitted with mini ballast ploughs, which seem to enhance the appearance of the locomotive. 20 September 1998.

Approaching Carrog station, nose to nose ex-BR Class 20s Nos 20020 and 20142 arrive with a late afternoon train from Llangollen during a Diesel Gala weekend. No. 20020 in BR green livery was visiting the railway from the Bo'ness & Kinneil Railway, which is where it ended up after withdrawal by British Rail in 1990 after thirty-one years' service on the main line. The locomotive was one of 228 built at Robert Stephenson & Hawthorn Ltd, Darlington, or the Vulcan Foundry between 1957 and 1968. 4 July 1999.

The author makes no apologies for showing another image of No. 25313 as she was a popular but useful locomotive at the railway. On this occasion, the Class 25 is hauling a typical mid-1970s mixed freight train as she gets ready to depart from the east end of Llangollen Goods Junction before heading into Llangollen station on 31 March 2003.

A view looking west towards Llangollen Goods Junction, taken from Abbey Road, with the shed yard line in the foreground. Ex-BR Class 37 No. 37240 in civil engineers' livery makes the final approach to Llangollen station on 7 June 2003 with an engineers' train. No. 37240 – a product of English Electric's Vulcan Foundry in 1964 (as D6940) – arrived at the railway in July 2002 after being withdrawn by EWS in 1999.

Ex-BR Sulzer Class 46 No. 46010 departs Carrog station with a midday train to Llangollen on 15 October 2000 as part of the Diesel Gala weekend. No. 46010 was built at Derby Works in 1962 as D147 before being renumbered in late 1973, and was withdrawn from traffic in 1984. It languished for a further nine years before being purchased by the Llangollen Diesel Group in 1993 and restored to full working order a few weeks before this image was taken.

Having being hauled out from the shed yard by Yorkshire Engine Co. 0-4-0 diesel No. 2854 (built in 1961), Class 47 No. 47449 makes its first appearance in its splendid two-tone BR green with its original number of D1566. This locomotive would have had a similar appearance in the late 1960s and early 1970s, before being repainted into BR corporate blue livery. 5 May 2002.